Making Therapy Work

Michael Schlein, LCPC

ISBN-13: 978-1546857235
ISBN-10: 1546857230

AUTHOR'S NOTE

The case profiles described in this book are composites of typical client stories. Some stories have been combined or partially fabricated, names and other identifying details have been altered to protect the privacy of the individual.

Table of Contents

For FREE articles and updates on Therapy, Growing, and Healing, visit my website at www.HowToMakeTherapyWork.Com or Email me directly at MakingTherapyWork@gmail.com

INTRODUCTION

CLIENTS: THE UNSUNG HEROES OF THERAPY

Congratulations! You made the decision to start your therapeutic journey, and that means you are on your way to a better life.

Once upon a time, there was a stigma about going to therapy. You had to be crazy to go to a therapist. Nowadays, you'd have to be crazy not to! Therapy is about healing pain, developing your emotional world, facing life transitions, and growing in confidence. If you are seeking to improve your life, therapy can provide the setting and structure to pursue your ideal life, break through limiting beliefs that are blocking you, and achieve an overall greater sense of well-being!

How can you get the most out of therapy so that you can live a life that's real, vibrant and connected to people you love and who love you?

As a therapist specializing in treating anxiety, depression and trauma, I've been educated by hundreds of hours of training, supervision, and consultation. I discovered that despite all my training and education about how to be a good therapist, no one was educating my clients and helping them make the most of their therapy.

Once I realized this, I began to incorporate this education as an integral part of the work that I do. The feedback I received from my clients was consistently positive and I found that it also supported the process of their therapy to progress and ultimately help them get the most from their therapy.

One session, a client and I were having a discussion about the process of therapy and her contribution as a client. At the end of this rewarding discussion, she asked me, "How come no one ever told me this before?" This client had a history of going to many therapists and no one had ever engaged her in this kind of discussion, explaining to her the important role of the client.

I challenged her and asked, "How come you never researched it yourself?" She responded that, in fact, she had looked into it many times, but never found anything clear and helpful on the topic. After the session, I did my own research and saw that she was correct. There was a gaping hole in the available resources that left clients without good guidance on how to make their therapy effective and explain how it works.

I was then inspired to write this book for all my future clients, and for anyone else who was braving through the journey of therapy.

How do you know if your therapist is any good? Is my therapy working? Am I doing it right or wasting my time? What exactly is therapy? Am I doing this right?

These are some of the common questions that many people consider when they begin therapy. To be sure, research shows that therapy does work. It helps make people's lives better, and more satisfying. But the reality is, therapy still seems to be working better for some people than others. Why some people seem to fly by with success in therapy while others don't benefit at all? How can you be sure to be making the most of your therapy?

I set out to research about what type of therapies and therapists offer the best and most efficient services, and what I found was truly eye-opening. While it's true that there are some therapists that are better than others, and some therapies that are better than others, it's also true that **there are some clients that 'do therapy' more effectively than others.**

Some people just seem to be more effective participants in therapy than others. There are certain clients that catch on very quickly in the therapy process, participate, and reap benefits; while there are others who either catch on slowly or all-together don't get it.

In a comprehensive research review of the role of clients in psychotherapy, Bohart and Tallman concluded that the Client, not the therapist, plays the biggest role in how well therapy works. In fact, internationally recognized expert in the field of psychotherapy research Dr. David Orlinsky (2004) concludes that the client is the "most determinant of outcome" in therapy.

In other words, whether you go to the most experienced and trained therapist or the newest and most novice, what you as the Client do in therapy and how you approach your own work makes the biggest difference!

This is great news for you because it means you really are in a position to play a positive role in getting the recovery and help you want. The advice and guidance available to you in this book is the synthesis of what we have learned from research combined with my experience as a therapist. Discovering this research was even more encouraging for me to write this book and make it available to everyone in therapy.

In this book, you will learn how to make the most of your therapy so that you can grow, change, and live a meaningful and full life. Good therapy improves the quality of life, and when you know how to **make therapy work**, then everything in life gets better!

Let me show you how!

CHAPTER 1

HEALING YOURSELF IN THERAPY AND LIFE

Before we attempt to understand how to grow and heal in therapy, let's take a look at why we don't naturally heal ourselves when we get stuck.

There may be several reasons that Clients often do not recognize that they are the most important factor in therapy and their own recovery. One almost-universal reason is that often the events that happened in the story of one's life that brought one to therapy to begin with are events that have left the client with a sense of disempowerment, submissiveness, and inadequacy.

It is the nature of that very wound that sets into motion a pattern of passivity that prevents an individual from seeing just how competent and capable they are. This is the reason why so many people seeking therapy struggle with self-confidence which creates a self-perpetuating cycle.[1]

Healing Yourself- Healing Your *Self*

Perhaps, being the one to heal yourself is greater than the healing itself. The very recognizing of your own role in your recovery and life is the first and possibly most important task in the therapeutic journey. In order to take full ownership in one's therapy, one needs to overcome those tendencies towards powerlessness, submissiveness and inadequacy moving instead towards self-reliance, confidence, and empowerment.

Powerlessness ⟶ Empowerment

Submissive ⟶ Self-Reliance

Inadequate ⟶ Confident

Common Mistakes About How Therapy Works

There are three common ways and beliefs through which clients undermine their crucial role in the therapy and the change process- all lodged in the context of the overall sense of disempowerment and inadequacy discussed above. The three ways are as follows:

1. The Therapist Will Fix Me

2. Showing Up to Therapy

3. Asking Advice

---

[1] At the end of the book I included an important insight about achievable Self-Confidence.

Let's take a closer look at these misconceptions and the truth about good therapy.

The Therapist Will Fix Me

How many therapists does it take to change a lightbulb?

One cannot change the lightbulb; it must change itself.

When therapy works, it's the client, not the therapist, that is the one who made it happen. This is consistent with what the Tao Te Ching says, "A leader is best when people barely know he exists, when his work is done, his aim fulfilled, they will say: **we did it ourselves.**"

Consider the following example:

Jay was a 24 year old client who came into therapy because he had a hard time in his dating life. He was known to be picky, but Jay explained that he simply never met a girl that he connects with. Jay's first few sessions he spoke about how the "women nowadays" don't appreciate an artistic romantic man. The next few sessions, Jay spoke about how his parents never encouraged him to be social, and he was always ashamed to be proactive in pursuing friendships. Three subsequent sessions were dedicated to Jay's criticism of the way his siblings got married to people totally not their type. Finally, Jay started the next session saying he was all done therapy, because he finally figured things out. Surprised (to say the least), I asked him to explain how therapy was helpful. He explained, "I finally got the message you were trying to get across to me. It's not about all the people I blame, I have to start taking responsibility for my own life. Thanks for helping me figure that out!"

The truth is, I never intended that message for Jay, nor did we ever talk about it. Jay reached this realization on his own simply by being allowed the space to explore his own thoughts and talk about it, and then finally having the opportunity to hear himself.

Therapeutic Hopelessness

Because most people enter therapy with the mindset that the therapist will do something for them either as the agent of change or expert adviser, it is quite often that about 5-8 weeks into therapy the client gets frustrated with either the therapist or therapy. Talking about this frustration is an important topic to bring up directly with your therapist.

This frustration is not because you are doing therapy wrong, nor is it proof that your therapist is lousy. In fact, it's most likely that you have just arrived at the first milestone in therapy. Recognizing the disappointment that the therapist can't just help you or do it for you is a powerful experience of realizing that in fact healing can't and won't come from outside of you, but that you will somehow have to heal yourself.

Recognizing this may initially cause you to feel sad and hopeless. However, what usually emerges from this hopelessness is the understanding that you are back in charge. This is the beginning of self-ownership.

One client coined a term for this and called it, "Therapeutic

Hopelessness." Although this hopelessness will make you feel sad at first, it presents a therapeutic opportunity because in order to be ready to take ownership of your own healing, you first have to let go of false hope that someone else can do it for you. Letting go of that false hope can help to rinse away feelings of inferiority and inspire you with a sense of capability and potential.

Fostering Therapeutic Hopelessness

The fact that you, and not the therapist, are the agent of change should be somewhat intuitive when you think about it. After all, how could any expert be able to change you on their own? However, despite how obvious this should be, many people tend to naturally wait for the therapist to do something and get frustrated when nothing happens.

Two questions that can help redirect the focus on you is to ask yourself, "In my wildest imagination, what could the therapist do that would actually change things for me? Would it work?"

Usually asking these question is sufficient to be in touch with the fact that no one outside of you can do the work of changing for you. Exploring this with your therapist can be especially helpful in this process.

A very common example in therapy can be illustrated by a session with a 26 year old female client named Julie. Julie had been in therapy with about 7 therapists and had established a track record of leaving the therapist, feeling disappointed despite not being able to identify exactly what could have been different. During one session, Julie shared with her therapist that she was getting increasingly more annoyed at therapy. When she explored this with her therapist, she revealed that deep down, there was a part of her that just wanted to be hugged by her therapist.[2] The therapist neither gave her the hug nor refused to. Instead, the therapist asked her, "If I give you that hug, would it help?" Julie was surprised to even have been asked the question; she was bracing herself to be ridiculed and let down. Given the opportunity to think it through, Julie figured out quickly that part of her wanted the hug and felt that by not getting it she would never get the security she needed in order to heal. Nevertheless, another part of her understood that getting a hug from her therapist wouldn't actually provide her the security she yearned for.

Deep down she had hoped that the therapist would heal her in some way. Julie learned that this only contributed to her sense of powerlessness, and that she intuitively understood that even the hug she had been longing for wasn't going to heal her. Instead, she needed to learn to provide herself with security. Her therapist was then able to help her learn skills to compliment her new mindset of wanting to provide her own sense of security.

---

[2] The Client desire for a hug or some other form of affection from the therapist is common in therapy and can sometimes feel quite intense. In fact, it's usually a good sign that a healthy therapeutic bond being created because it indicates that you've formed a connection to someone who is caring and safe. However, it's really important that your therapist practice good boundaries within the guidelines of their professional ethics codes. A therapist without boundaries is a red flag.

Julie's story highlights another very common theme that shows up in therapy. One of the reasons that people get stuck is because they are hopeful in something that can't happen. For example, when a child is denied basic love, affection and security that is necessary to develop a strong sense of self, the child often avoids feeling despair by putting their hope in receiving that love and security from someone else. This desire to be mothered by others persists into adulthood. Unfortunately, when the child becomes an adult, they discover that other adults are neither interested nor capable of being their mother or father. This leaves the adult child of neglect feeling unlovable and endlessly seeking security from others.

In therapy, the individual can uncover this subconscious agenda and reevaluate what may be a more achievable goal. Once an unconscious drive is made conscious, a person is in the position to change it or respond to it constructively. They can choose alternatives that allow them to let go of their hope, while not falling into despair.

There are two common responses to this discovery that put a person on the path to healing. One response is to mourn the loss of what they never had and will never get. The second response is to discover that they have inner resources within them that that they can use to provide security for themselves in a way that they didn't have when they were younger.

In this way, the "therapeutic hopelessness" of discovering that they can't just replace childhood unmet needs with modern artificial substitutes opens up the door to possibilities of finding reasonable solutions.

Showing Up to Therapy

A second way we forget to take responsibility in therapy is expressed in the language we use when we say "I go to therapy." Some clients literally just show up because they think or were told, "you need to go to therapy." And that's exactly what they do. They go- that's it. Spoiler: It doesn't work.

I recently heard that 80% of gym income comes from people who pay membership, but don't actually show up. In therapy, there's no membership, so no one actually pays without showing up physically; but many clients certainly show up and then don't actually *do therapy*.

Therapy doesn't work by itself, it is the setting where you can do work that will help you. It's no different than going to the gym. You won't lose weight or get stronger by just showing up and staring at all the equipment. Unless you are actually using the equipment and breaking a sweat, nothing will change, no matter how much money you spend on the membership and no matter how talented your personal trainer is.

This type of attitude actually works pretty well when you go to the medical doctor. You just show up and report your symptoms, and the doctor makes a diagnosis and prescribes treatment. It doesn't really require much from you except willingness and compliance.

In therapy, the client has to be much more active in their recovery at every level. This involves thinking about what you want to talk about, exploring what you don't want to talk about, and creating your own vision of what you want your goals to be. Therapy is a collaborative process and requires that you talk to your therapist about your goals, and even what type of treatment you would like to try. Often, clients hesitate to tell the therapist that they want to do things differently. However, the truth is that your therapist would LOVE if you gave your opinion more often. Without communicating what you like and what works for you, your therapist is likely to get it wrong from time to time, and as a result the therapy won't be helping you as well as it otherwise could.

At the same time, you may have an idea that won't necessarily be the best choice for you and it's important to be open to hearing feedback from your therapist. The key is keeping the therapy a collaborative process.

In the upcoming chapters, we will describe in more detail exactly what it means to "do the work" of good therapy. First, let's cover the last of the three common ways client's inadvertently interfere with their own therapy.

Asking Advice

The third common way a client unknowingly prevents himself from doing therapy effectively is by asking the therapist for advice. It's a mistake to assume that the therapist is some guru or expert like Dr. Phil that somehow knows better than the client how to live life. To be abundantly clear, it's a mistake to think that anyone is such an expert.

To be sure, when you are asking advice from someone else, it expresses your desire to change and seek options for growth. This represents a willingness to be influenced by others in a positive way and a healthy motivation to be active. That's great! While this is a step better than the passivity of the client who just shows up, it's still not enough to make therapy work. Asking advice can be a helpful thing to do when you just want to hear another person's perspective as a way of helping you work through your own thought process. However, all-too-often, clients tend to be handing over the controls of their lives to the therapist and asking What-Should-I-Do type of questions. Even though this comes from a genuine motivation to change, it still can reinforce the powerlessness that is the very nature of the original wound that keeps the you stuck in life.

Part of the reason that clients seek advice is because of misconceptions they have about the role of the therapist. Another common cause for this inclination to ask for advice often stems from previous experiences in the client's life when the client was given the implicit message that he isn't capable of making his own decision and that someone else is more authoritative than he. Consider the following example:

Hanna was a 32 year old female who was a successful teacher and had a great reputation as a professional. Despite being attractive and having been romantically involved with several men who expressed a wish to marry her, Hanna declined. When Hanna came in for her first appointment, she quickly gave me her history and said she wanted to get straight to the point. "I'm dating a guy named Jeremy now that I really like, for the first time in my life I met someone that I really want to marry. My father said that he doesn't want me marrying him because Jeremy doesn't make a lot of money, and my father said he thinks I can do better. I just don't know what to do!" I listened to her, and couldn't help but feel like screaming, "Marry him! Let your father deal with his own issues!" I reminded myself that I am sitting across from a highly intelligent and accomplished woman and that even though she is asking for my advice, she is really capable of making this decision on her own. And so I said, "Yikes. What do you plan on doing?" Hanna looked at me dumbfounded and said, "Well, um, this is what I plan on doing. I'm asking you." I told her that I was surprised that she would ask me advice on living her life, after all, I don't even know her. Hanna began to get frustrated with my not giving her advice and asked, "What am I paying you so much money for if you're not giving me advice?!" I responded, "I have no idea why you'd pay me so much money to tell you how to live your life when you have your father doing that for free." At that point, Hanna just slumped in her seat and continued ruminating in her plight. She left the session clearly disappointed.

A week later I received a text from Hanna with a picture of her, a handsome looking fellow, and a caption that said, "Yay! This is a picture of me and my Fiancé Jeremy! Thank you for everything! After I left your office, I felt disappointed in you. Then I realized, you didn't give me advice because you believed in me. I don't think I ever got that from anyone before. That was exactly what I needed. Thank you!"

Be your own authority over your life! If you think others may have insight or intelligence to offer you, then be humble enough to consult with them. But ultimately, your life is yours, and only you can live it. After consulting others, turn inward, and consult your own intuition. Listening to your own intuition is a way of claiming ownership of your life and sets you on the path to healing.

Therapy Is Hard Work

In preparing to write this book, I took a survey of people who were either formerly or currently clients in therapy and asked them what they would recommend to someone who just started therapy and wants to make the most of it. The majority of them said as their first answer, "It's hard work, but worth it."

What exactly is entailed in this hard work? The next three chapters are dedicated to offering specific advice to help guide you in doing the "hard work" that makes therapy "worth it."

CHAPTER 2

HOW THERAPY WORKS

A famous psychologist once commented, "When the therapist is working harder than the client, it's not therapy." When asking experienced therapists to reflect on the qualities of clients who succeeded the most in their therapy, most therapists will enthusiastically say right off the bat, "Motivated and active!" Everyone who shows up to therapy has some sort of motivation, but there are some clients that seem motivated yet aren't as active in the actual process of therapy.

In order to understand what it means to be active in the therapy process, it helps to understand what exactly therapy is and how it helps. While a comprehensive analysis of this is way beyond the scope of this book , let's take a closer look at one aspect of this together.

Every person has a host of human drives that motivate and direct him in life. The drive for Connection and the drive for Significance are examples of these natural drives. There are two other drives that are both strong and yet conflicting: the drive to feel satisfied and proud of the way you are, and the drive to grow and aspire for more.

Life is the journey of pursuing, negotiating, and sometimes dancing between many conflicting drives. The greatest struggle in this pursuit is how to balance the tension between these conflicting drives to stay the same and to grow.

At every stage of life, one is driven to sit back and stay the same with a sense of having arrived at accomplishment and achievement. At the same time he is motivated to begin a new journey.

When something happens that one experiences as too painful to accept and yet too powerful to overcome, one can easily get stuck because both of these drives have been neutralized. Hence, he experiences some state of powerlessness or inadequacy. Because it is too painful, it is too hard to allow his drive to stay the same to compel him to accept the situation. On the other hand, because it is too powerful and overwhelming, his drive to grow and change also doesn't compel him at that moment either. And thus he becomes stuck.

At a psychologically challenging juncture such as this, the person has only two options. He may either lose all drive and shut down emotionally or he may avoid accepting his reality in a desperate attempt to preserve his drives and vitality. In the case of the latter, he essentially tells himself a lie in return for a façade of life being fine and him being ok. This allows him to believe that everything is fine, however it doesn't change the reality that he was truly overwhelmed to the point of being disempowered. In a way, this lie is the product of his drive to remain the same, but at the expense of his drive to grow. The result is that he is forced to shut down his drive for growth and instead live a life of always just settling. Ultimately, when this happens, he will develop a tell-tale pattern of being stuck in life. Consider the following example:

> Hank, an 18 year old male, was referred to therapy by his older brother who saw Hank was having a hard time making decisions and seemed to be in turmoil about what direction to take in life. During the intake session, Hank said he was never abused, and considers the biggest traumatic incident in his life the time he couldn't go on the 11th grade overnight trip with his class. After several months of exploring his inner world in therapy, Hank expressed he was nervous that he "wasn't meant to ever grow up." He would like to stay in the comfort of childhood forever. When I asked him if he remembers ever being a child and wishing he were an adult, Hank just sat there staring into space, his face turning pale. After several moments of silent contemplation, he looked up said, "I know what this is about." The next session, Hank described a time when he was about 11 years old and an older boy in his neighborhood sexually abused him. As is often the case when a child feels the shame inherent in sexual abuse, Hank never told anyone. He told himself, "It's not such a big deal; I can handle it. How would telling an adult help anyway, I can

handle this as well as an adult. In fact, it doesn't affect me, I'm too mature to let it get to me."

In Hank's desperate attempt to avoid the pain and hurt of the sexual abuse, he detached from his experience and instead attached himself to the idea that he was unaffected, and didn't need to work through anything. Instead, he convinced himself that he was OK the way he was.

Once Hank had let in the truth of how overwhelmed and helpless he had been, he was able to work through the feelings of shame and vulnerability. Therapy helped him do this, as well as develop feelings of security and safety. From this place of safety, Hank embarked on his next stage in life, and finally he had the confidence to make decisions about his own future.

This balance between remaining the same vs. growing requires the depth of inner reflection and thoughtful contemplation of the individual person. No guru can give advice to spare you from going through this yourself. The upside is that it is very rewarding work!

Therapy is a place with certain environmental conditions that help a person understand his life's story, and inner world so that he can explore how he has arrived where he is, and to where he wants to go next. A skilled therapist is the main object in this environment that helps the client do all this successfully. It takes bravery to face difficult feelings and memories. Reality can be harsh. A good therapist isn't afraid to gently support you and guide you to looking at what you may have been avoiding.

What is a healthy way to reconcile the conflict between the drive to accept yourself as you are now and the drive to grow and change? How does Therapy provide that?

The Paradox of Change

Carl Rogers, perhaps the most influential therapist of all time, described the therapy process and said, "The curious paradox is that when I accept myself just as I am, then I change."

Rogers, in a most succinct and perhaps poetic way, was addressing the issue that directly trying to change oneself through effort and force doesn't work. Instead, change is only possible through accepting yourself. Sometimes throughout life, it's painful to accept one's self or something that happened to oneself and so in our attempt to avoid that pain we act as if we have somehow reached the end without needing to do the work to get there.

Only through fully accepting oneself and one's story can we truly arrive at ourselves, and then begin the next Journey. Brene Brown, Social Science Researcher and Author of Daring Greatly, wrote the following very powerful perspective:

"Owning our story can be hard but not nearly as difficult as spending our lives running from it. Embracing our vulnerabilities is risky but not nearly as dangerous as giving up on love and belonging and joy—the experiences that make us the most vulnerable. Only when we are brave enough to explore the darkness will we discover the infinite power of our light."

In other words, fully accepting yourself and your situation empowers you to grow and change your situation.

Therapy As a Laboratory For Life

The process of therapy is a process of both acceptance and change. At many stages of therapy, the client is not explicitly engaged in trying to make changes. Instead, the client, with the help of the therapist, embarks to fully explore himself and accept himself and his life. The result of this acceptance is change.

The cornerstone of all therapy is empathy and validation. This does not mean that the therapist will just tell you whatever you want to hear and tell you that you are right. At times, that would just be enabling you to avoid the truth. Instead, the therapist uses empathy and validation when appropriate to help you get in touch with your experience- whatever it may be.

At other times, the therapist will actually challenge you to explore feelings and memories you may otherwise not want to. Although this doesn't usually feel good initially, it helps a person accept himself; and nothing feels better than living one's own truth.

Self-Acceptance As An End

Another reason that self-acceptance is an important therapeutic task is because self-acceptance and learning to be yourself is an essential key to well being. Eckart Tolle, author of The Power of Now, wrote: "You find peace not by rearranging the circumstances of your life, but by realizing who you are at the deepest level."

In therapy, being at the change stage usually means either considering making actual changes in your life or participating in a technique that the therapist is suggesting.

For example, a common technique that many therapists teach their clients is a skill called Cognitive Restructuring. The goal of Cognitive Restructuring is to actively change thoughts or beliefs that are negatively affecting the way you feel or behave. This is not in conflict to accepting yourself the way you are, but a proactive response to it! In engaging in this type of activity, you are not just changing something about yourself, but also developing a greater sense of Self as you grow in self-mastery.

Oftentimes change happens without needing any active skill or technique. The very exploring of yourself with self-compassion allows unconscious thoughts and feelings to emerge, and once they become conscious they can finally be let go.

Concluding Thought

Understanding the process of therapy is essential in order to get the most out of it. While the goal of therapy is to facilitate change, pursuing that change before first working towards accepting where you are and how you got there can actually sabotage the change process. When you approach therapy as an opportunity to pursue both Self-acceptance and change, it not only makes the therapy more effective for the specific change you are seeking, but it also empowers you to manage life more successfully when you complete therapy. In this way, therapy doesn't make you weaker, it makes you stronger!

So here's the takeaway: The goal of therapy is change, but the primary objective of therapy is curious exploration and non-judgmental self-acceptance.

CHAPTER 3

MAKING THERAPY WORK

Now that you understand the process of therapy, how do you become an active motivated client so that you can get the most out of your time and money in therapy and achieve the positive changes you've been wanting?

According to the research, one of the biggest predictors of successful therapy is an active client. This requires being proactive both in and out of therapy. In the next chapter, we'll discuss what you can do outside of the therapy session that will help; in this chapter we'll describe what it means to be active during the session itself.

As described in the previous chapter, while the goal of therapy is to help facilitate a change of some sort, the objective of the therapy session is often to work on self-acceptance and exploration. Any active participation you make to explore your self will go a long way in helping your therapy be a success!

Willingness to Explore the Uncomfortable

Often, one of the things that stops us from exploring our inner world is that it's uncomfortable. For example, when a person is experiencing the discomfort of anxiety, they are primarily interested in getting rid of that feeling and therefore much prefer to seek out ways of relaxing than to explore the anxiety. Likewise, when someone is feeling depressed, their reflex is to seek a "cure" that will make them feel better. Understandably, they prefer not to explore the very feeling that is causing them pain.

However, it's really important to understand that our emotions, even the seemingly negative ones, are there for a reason and the pains we feel are signals to us to turn towards them and understand them. Often they are either calling us to action or simply asking to be understood. Just knowing this helps attune us to the therapeutic process of acceptance and exploration without getting carried away by the reflex to change them immediately.

So the first thing you can do to make your sessions more rewarding is bring awareness to your discomfort and willingness to tolerate it.

Prepare Before the Session to Talk and Explore

The most important thing you can do in therapy is come

prepared to talk and explore. Therapy can be a great opportunity just to talk even about things you know already. Sometimes, just speaking about it with another person helps you process your feelings, thoughts, and emotions in a healthier way than just knowing it.

Talking in therapy also helps put us in touch with what goes on in our inner world. Carl Rogers is quoted as saying, "How can I think before I speak? I don't even know what I'm thinking until I say it." Being heard in therapy helps us think about and organize our experiences.

Before you even come to the session, it's a good idea to think about what you want to speak about. This is something you can be thinking about throughout the week, or right before a session. Either way, you don't want to come straight into the session without having given consideration to how you want to take advantage of it.

Often, Clients want to know what they should talk about. Planning and staying focused in the therapy can be somewhat tricky at times. You should be talking about this openly with your therapist. The following are some guiding principles that you may find helpful.

Talk About What's On Your Mind

You want to talk about whatever is on your mind and feels significant to you. Most of the time, whatever is on your mind in the present moment has some relevant connection to what is at your core and what you want to work on.

> Kari came to therapy with the hope to reduce the fact that she was a "worry-bug" and had a hard time making any decisions- both important and trivial. One

particular session, after she had become familiar with the therapeutic process, Kari wanted to explore her indecisiveness about whether she should look into switching jobs so she could work closer to home. Initially, Kari just said, "I don't know what to do! I feel like I'm just going to end up staying where I am because I am not capable and strong enough to make decisions anyway!"

The therapist asked her to expand on what makes the decision unclear to her. Kari took advantage of the invitation to explore her indecisiveness and discovered that part of what was holding her back was that she didn't want to disappoint her current boss. Upon further introspection, Kari discovered that she was most afraid of hearing criticism from her boss. This discovery led Kari to realize that a lot of her indecisiveness in life is connected to a fear that others will criticize her for being self-serving. This made it virtually impossible for her to make decisions in her best interest because she harbored a fear that such a decision would reflect bad on her. Once Kari got in touch with this fear, she was able to release it by recognizing that her fear was more imagined than real. Moreover, she substituted a new belief that making decisions in her best interest doesn't make her self-serving, it makes her self-compassionate. For Kari, making decisions became a lot easier.

Kari's story is a great example of how talking about whatever is going on for you in life is a great path to finding what's going on for you at your core. For Kari, after uncovering this fear, she was able to own it and deal with it differently. For many, this simple insight is enough, while for others, it leads the

way to talking about how this fear developed and helps them look at the impact of their childhoods.

Of course, there is also advantage to taking into consideration creating continuity in your sessions. Sometimes it's worthwhile to put-off speaking about current events in your life in order to continue a topic or theme that's been relevant in therapy. When something big and disturbing is going on in your life, it would make sense to not ignore it and bring it into your sessions. However, there's also an advantage of being able to press pause on other things that are happening in your life in order to really attend to themes that would otherwise be neglected.

Imagine in one session you discover that you have a pervasive pattern of not believing other people really want to connect with you. In this session, you come to both identify this pattern and recognize that it plays a big role in the hopeless you feel in social situations. It would make sense that the next session you should start off by revisiting this topic, perhaps to regain focus on it and continue exploring it. Alternatively, you may provide an update in terms of how you continued processing this point after last session and what work you have done on your own.

By taking an active role in creating continuity in the session content, you also build bridges from the session to your week. This allows you to maintain focus on your goals and the process of therapy without feeling like you have to randomly talk about whatever is happening in your schedule.

Now, you may ask, "So am I supposed to talk about whatever is on my mind, or am I supposed to talk about what we did last week?"

This is somewhat of a trick question. This question puts a lot of emphasis on what you are supposed to do and does not put enough importance on your role to decide what's important to you. To be sure, therapy helps most when both criteria are met. That is, you talk about what is important to you and maintain a focus from session to session. Of course, if you find there is a recurrence of talking about what is important to you and it is not with therapeutic focus, your therapist may point out to you that you seem to be getting distracted. This is not a criticism but rather an important aspect to explore. Is it possible that although you want to change something in particular you also have a part of you that is distracting you?

However, when a client is struggling to understand exactly what she is *supposed* to talk about in therapy, there is a certain dynamic emerging of her trying to do things right instead of doing things her way. Perhaps she is giving too much importance to her performance as a client, perhaps she is attributing too much authority to the therapist, or perhaps she is just not looking inward to her intuition about what is important to her.[3] Whatever the reason, ultimately deciding what to talk about in therapy is an important role for the client to take upon herself. It demonstrates and contributes to the development of agency and autonomy.

In Affect Regulation Theory, Dan Hill compares the client's taking the lead position in therapy to set the topics and goals based on subjective self-determination to the emergence of the *self* in infancy. He describes this as being the milestone of successful therapy and writes, "At some point patients begin

---

[3] This is similar to the roots of perfectionism when a person avoids performing at a personal subjective standard and instead tries to achieve according to some objective standard that is sourced somewhere external.

to work differently. They are not simply telling things to and expecting things of the therapist. Rather, they begin a free-associative process of voluntarily letting the mind go where it goes, think what it things, feel what it feels."

Whose Line Is It Anyway?

What is actually discussed and spoken about during a session is important. Equally important is who begins the conversation at the start of the session.

There are differences between various therapy approaches as to how directive the role of the therapist should be. Some therapists will check in at the beginning of every session and remind the client what was spoken about last week and make a suggestion as to how that conversation can be continued in the new session. In contrast, in classic depth-therapy, the client starts the session. In fact, traditional psychoanalysts will not even greet with "hello." Whatever the style of your therapist, for therapy to work, it has to be *your* therapy.

Harry Stack Sullivan once said, "If the therapist is working harder than the patient, it's not therapy." In order to make therapy yours, you have to be working on goals that are important to you and talking about topics that are important to you. Whether or not your therapist begins by greeting you and asking about your week, to get the most of your therapy it would probably be a good idea for you to show initiative in your session by directing it towards what you want to talk about.

Likewise, you may find yourself in the middle of a conversation with your therapist and start to feel like you are not talking about what you really want to. It can feel kind of awkward because you are stuck talking about it, but don't really want to be. Remember: therapy parallels your life. If you don't want to stay stuck in a rut in life, then it starts with learning to work through small awkward situations like this in therapy. Playing an active role in your therapy and even stopping the flow midway so that you can redirect it in the direction that will help you is all part of learning to be more proactive in your life and taking ownership of it.

You might be thinking, "The therapist is the expert, and I should just follow his lead." It's important to remember that even the best therapists are human. They cannot always know how their interactions with you are impacting you and certainly they cannot know what your needs, values and goals are without you establishing them and pursuing them throughout the therapy process. Sometimes, a therapist may inadvertently impose his own goals for you onto you. This does not necessarily mean that he is a bad therapist, it just means he is human. How you balance following his guidance without submitting to his desire for you in therapy will be a major factor in how successful your therapy is.

The following are some common signs that you may have surrendered your power in therapy and let the habit of submissiveness contaminate therapy:

- You intuitively know that the topic you are discussing is not relevant to you, but you just go along with it
- You show up not knowing what to talk about
- You ask for advice or your therapist offers it
- The dialogue feels more like an interview
- You don't understand why the topic has taken the direction it has

Not knowing what to talk about can create a sense of pressure. Ambiguity is stressful. But the truth is that the stress of ambiguity mixed with the pressure to push through it is exactly what energizes creativity. Tolerating this anxiety of Non-knowing is actually the bridge that connects a person to their own generativity and problem-solving ability. John Keats, the Romantic English poet of the 19th Century, suggested that the key to accessing creativity was honing a skill he termed Negative Capability. He wrote, "I mean Negative Capability, that is when man is capable of being in uncertainties, mysteries, doubts, without any irritable reaching after fact and reason." According to Keats, the capacity to tolerate the ambiguity of life being uncertain energizes creativity and the ability to imagine new perspectives.

It may feel anxiety provoking at first. To be sure, by definition good therapy will be somewhat anxiety provoking because the underlying mechanism of most therapy is to help you face experiences and opportunities that you have been avoiding. The good news is that it gets much easier. With practice and persistence you will learn the skill of self-reflection and find it rewarding to let go of looking for guidance from outside of you.

The big takeaway is this: you are the biggest expert on you. A skilled therapist can guide you in exploring yourself and help you get in touch with hidden layers of your experience. He may even be able to impart universal wisdom to you that can be helpful to know. But in the end of the day, only you can really access your experience to be in touch with your thoughts, beliefs, and feelings. Only you can determine your values and make decisions about how you want to be and what you want to do. A good therapist will affirm this and empower you.[4]

---

[4] See **Treating Complex Trauma and Dissociation** (Danylchuk): "That is not to say that the therapist has no power; the therapist has a lot of power, but the power the therapist has resides in authority based upon his or her expertise, knowledge, training and sensitivity. The point is to use this

Claiming ownership in life shows up in all matters- big and small. How you participate in therapy and how you start the session and direct it throughout represents your sense of self-sovereignty in your life. Therapy is a great place to start taking your life back as your own.

Letting Feelings In

It has almost become cliché that the most common question therapists ask is, "How does that make you feel?" The reason for this is because feelings are really the portal to self-reflection and personal experience.

Exploring feelings can be very difficult for a number of reasons. It's easy to just ignore your personal experience and focus on the external content of what is happening in the world. It's a lot harder to shift that focus to what is happening in your inner world.

One of the reasons that talking about emotions is so hard is because it can be really uncomfortable. This is especially true when the emotions are negative such as feelings of being hurt, insulted, violated, and unloved. Often, we try to block out these feelings, but they never go away. Another strategy people try to do to dampen the impact of the negative feeling is to talk about it in an intellectual way, without letting in the experience.

The success of your therapy has a lot to do with the level of willingness you have to let in your experience even with negative emotions. Talking about how things in your life, both present and past, impact you emotionally opens you up to

---

authority in a way in which the client can also begin to feel his or her own authority, and begin to develop a healthy feeling of power. The word used quite often now is "empowerment." How do you empower a client?"

experience it in ways you cannot do without speaking about it.

Humans are wired to experience life socially. That means that in order to really take in an experience, even a very personal individual experience, you need to be willing to talk about it with another person who is capable of creatively listening and witnessing. This is another reason why therapy works with a trained and experienced therapist, even if they aren't your closest friend or family member.

Willingness to Try Therapy-type Talk

The type of talk that goes on in therapy isn't necessarily the same type of talk that goes on between friends. Usually with friends, they respond to what you say at the same level of experience that you expressed it. In therapy, the therapist is trained to help you get in touch with your experience in a deeper way than you already are. In order to do this, the therapist might ask you a question or guide you in an exercise that would seem rather awkward in a different social context. Bringing a willingness to try new things in therapy will go a long way in making it a successful experience.

When It's Hard To Talk About "It"

One stumbling block about choosing what to speak about in therapy that comes up a lot is that certain events are so difficult to talk about that it feels like you can't talk about them. This inability can be real and actually manifests at the neurological level in such a way that it really is impossible to talk about at first, and can't be overcome with force. At times like this, some clients make the mistake of not bringing it up at all. However, this is still something you want to bring up with your therapist.

Sometimes the therapist can help use techniques like EMDR in a way that doesn't require talking about, or Sandtray therapy which is a very powerful non-verbal modality. At other times, it can be helpful just to talk about why you're not talking about it.

Whenever you are not sure what to speak about, it's always good to talk about that with your therapist. Your therapist's job isn't to convince you that you should speak about it, but he may help you explore why you are not talking about it. From experience I can tell you that it's worth exploring even if you never end up talking about the actual event.

Shifting Focus Off the Symptoms

One of the things every therapist is good at is getting to the root of the problem. Most of the time, clients come in to therapy because of a specific symptom, like anxiety. The client doesn't want the anxiety and wants to work on it directly. Sometimes, just a few relaxation techniques and the awareness that you need to take time for yourself is enough to abate the anxiety.

However, quite often, anxiety is just a symptom of something going on beneath the surface, and spending longer time exploring this in therapy can be helpful. Some therapists tend to focus on childhood experiences and how they shaped your personality. Other therapists focus less on childhood but still explore broader aspects of your personality that may be contributing to your symptoms. It's important to be willing to explore beyond just the symptoms in order to get to the root of the problem.

Part of shifting focus off of the symptoms means focusing less on the outcome and more on the process of your own experience. Good therapy results in good outcomes. However, part of good therapy is focusing on the process and not just the outcome. Whether you are struggling with anxiety, depression, compulsive behavior, or relationship issues, the objective of therapy will include developing an ability to self-reflect, communicate, and respond to difficult emotions. Focusing on these processes helps to make therapy work.

Talk About the Therapy

There's probably nothing that can help to make your therapy more effective than talking about it with your therapist. Whether you are feeling stuck, or just have nothing else to talk about, talking about the therapy itself always proves to be an effective way of moving things along. One reason for this is because practicing good communication is the only way to really form a collaborative relationship with your therapist. Many people never had an opportunity to work with someone else in a way they felt comfortable expressing their opinions and disappointments. Therapy is supposed to give you this opportunity as a learning experience.

Some clients hear this and get worried they will sound ungrateful to their therapist or fear that the therapist will react defensively. In order for therapy to work well, you need to know you are with another person who cares about you and takes you seriously. If the therapist can't handle hearing your honest and open concerns about the experience you are having with therapy, I believe it's better you find that out earlier than later because it most likely means they are not the best fit for you.

Silence Is Golden

In daily conversation outside of the therapy context, you use words to express something you feel or know. In therapy, by contrast, talking is not just to express something you know but a way of discovering what is going on inside. Often, until you have an opportunity to talk about it with someone who listens without judgment, you don't actually understand what's going on in your mind.

During this process it happens that there are times that as you are talking or answering a question, you become aware of something deep coming up for you. If you feel that you can share your discovery with your therapist as it emerges, then go ahead and do so. Often, however, at times like this you are faced with a dilemma. If you attempt to share it immediately, it seems to escape you as words don't quite capture the emotional experience. When this happens, I suggest you try using silence as a way to make space for whatever is coming up. Don't be shy to just sit there in silence greeting your new awareness. The same way therapists are trained to talk about things in a different way than you would normally find in a conversations with friends, they are also used to sitting in silence when it's part of your exploration process.

CHAPTER 4

MOTIVATION TO MAKE THERAPY WORK

Goals vs. Motivation

Many people will tell you that it is important to have a goal in therapy. To be more precise, having a goal is not as important as having a motivation. As discussed above, focusing too much on a goal and desired outcome can actually be counter-productive. Instead, having a motivation and will is the most central element that drives therapy to success. A goal is *what* you want, but a motivation is *why* and *how* you want it.

Psychotherapy researchers have made a distinction between two types of motivation and have determined that when it comes to successful therapy, not all motivations are created equal. People who enter therapy with *intrinsic motivation* have a higher rate of achieving desired outcome than people who enter therapy with *extrinsic motivation*.[5]

---

[5] In fact, people motivated by intrinsic motivation in all their endeavors in life are happier, more successful and productive that people motivated by

Intrinsic motivation refers to an individual being motivated by a drive or need that emerges from them and with which they personally identify. In contrast, extrinsic motivation refers to an individual who is motivated by an externally imposed incentive or threat from outside of the person. Common examples of clients who enter therapy with extrinsic motivation include teenagers who are forced by parents to go to therapy because of behavioral concerns or court ordered clients who are told that they require therapy as part of their probation. In some cases, a person enters therapy on his own volition but yet still only engages in the process of therapy from a place of extrinsic motivation.

To illustrate this, consider the case of Laura, a client of 54 years old. Laura was referred by a couples therapist to do some individual work. According to Laura, she wanted to work on the fact that she was too rigid in her expectations and judgements of others. Her husband and children have complained that her constant nitpicking makes her presence burdensome and difficult to connect with. The therapist asked her if her critical nature and high-standards impacts her negatively and she said that if it were up to her, she wouldn't change anything about it. However, since it is bothering her family, she feels compelled to work on it.

For Laura, improving her marriage and relationships was an intrinsic motivation, however improving her character was only an extrinsic motivation. Therefore, even though she willingly opted to come to therapy and the level of her motivation was high, the quality of her motivation for the goal of becoming less

---

external motivations. (Pink, Drive). This is another example of therapy being a parallel process to a person's extra-therapeutic life.

critical of others was not sufficient. This made therapy difficult and unfortunately Laura initially made little progress towards her goal of becoming less critical.

One thing that may have been helpful to Laura is if her therapist had helped her find what her intrinsic motivation was that she could work on. For example, are there other things in her life that would have been more personally meaningful to her to work on? Alternatively, had she spent some more time giving attention to how her own critical nature went against her own best interest, she may have developed a greater sense of wanting to change it. In this way, she would have been able to develop her extrinsic motivation to the point that it became intrinsic.

What actually happened with Laura in her therapy is not so dissimilar from what many others experience when guided by a therapist. Upon closer exploration, there was a deeper significance to the fact that Laura resisted establishing her own intrinsic motivation for being in therapy. On the surface, Laura seemed to have a tough exterior and was not genuinely interested in changing her critical nature. However, the therapist helped Laura take a look beneath the surface and what she learned was that she had an established pattern of not asserting her own will and self-interest, and instead she assumed a passive stance when relating to others. In her initial moments of therapy, when she omitted having her own intrinsic will to change, she was unconsciously reenacting her pattern of remaining passive towards her own self-interest.

It's no wonder that Laura was known to be so critical of her close friends and family. Laura didn't know how to work on herself, see her role in her relationships, or even feel comfortable with her place in life. She was used to focusing on others and resented that at some level. Moreover, criticizing others made perfect sense because she was too helpless to work on herself.

Overtly, she claimed that she only came to therapy for others and that she herself had no intrinsic motivation. However, this absence of personal will revealed a covert presence of passivity- bearing witness to a woman who at some point in her life lost her power to have and assert her own will and care for self. For Laura, as is true for many individuals, establishing her own intrinsic motivation in therapy was not just necessary to make therapy work, but the healing itself. She was able to let herself matter more in her own motivations both in therapy and beyond. Over time she became more comfortable being proactive in her own best interest, which helped her learned to relate to others without criticizing them.

Motivation for the Therapeutic Task

In addition to looking at the outcome which you want to gain from therapy, it's important to consider your motivation and willingness to engage in the actual therapeutic task. Remember, the main task of therapy is self-reflection. Of course, self-reflection can be very rewarding both inherently and because it leads to change. However, reflecting on your own inner world of thoughts, feelings and beliefs is also very challenging. Naturally, we all have many automatic defenses that prevent and distract us from being able to effectively self-reflect. This is where a skilled therapist can be helpful to effectively engage in self-reflection while noticing and blocking defenses.

Consider Paul, a 55 year-old middle school teacher who came to therapy because he risked losing his job after building a reputation for losing his temper especially when disciplining students and saying not nice comments to them. Paul recognized that he had an "anger issue," and expected to work on "anger management." To be sure, Paul wasn't just afraid of losing his job (extrinsic motivation), he genuinely wanted to overcome his angry nature as he felt ashamed of the way he acted and really wanted to be a better teacher and person (intrinsic motivation). However, when it came to participating in the therapy, Paul found it cumbersome and unnecessary to engage in self-reflection and kept challenging the therapy process insisting that all he wanted was skills to help him control himself and not to look at his feelings. Intrinsic motivation was not enough for Paul to engage in therapy in a way that made it effective.

However, since he was truly motivated to gain more control of his actions and avoid losing his job, he stayed in therapy. The therapist continued to invite him to explore his feelings and over time, he learned to make more contact with his emotions. As things progressed, Paul developed a greater appreciation of the value of accepting his emotions and eventually garnered an intrinsic motivation to explore his inner life of thoughts and emotions. Ultimately, this allowed Paul to benefit from therapy in a way that he conquered his impulses for anger.

An additional dimension of the motivation and focus necessary to make therapy work is that therapy can only help with issues that are intrapsychic- meaning to say matters that concern your personal psychology, your mind, and your internal experience. In therapy you explore and shift how you feel about things, and how you feel about your feelings. You can make changes in your personality or your thinking that will affect how you deal with the circumstances in your life. All of the goals of therapy are exclusively about your own psychology and inner world.

The Role of Feelings in Therapy

"How does that make you feel?" Perhaps the biggest stereotype that people hear about therapy and therapist is that they always ask this question. Well, it's true and probably not changing.

For many, engaging in self-reflection and accepting the inner world of feelings comes naturally. However, for many others it doesn't come naturally and it can seem somewhat burdensome. Why bother trying to know yourself so deeply, doesn't it make more sense to just learn skills to make the anxiety go away or be more positive instead of depressed?

This question is only to be expected because honestly the work of looking inward is challenging and can bring up uncomfortable feelings. Moreover, the idea of just getting rid of the symptoms of anxiety and depression can be appealing because it is built on the understanding that the anxiety and depression have nothing to do with you. When we look for ways to banish our anxieties and disown them, we tell ourselves the lie that the anxiety is not really part of who we are, just an intrusive stranger who is trespassing our psychic lives. However, the truth is that much of the time, the parts of us we try to silence are the parts of us that need to be heard.

Anxiety is often a cue that you have been neglecting a drive inside of you that is calling you to action. Depression can be an indication that you are not living a life aligned with your values in a meaningful way or not fulfilling your potential. Imagine the opportunity that would be lost if instead of heeding the call of your feelings, you endeavor to quash it just to restore temporary relief. Even addictions and compulsive behaviors are often a misguided drive that needs to be understood and not just "fixed" and dispelled. Experts specializing in addictions have taught us that underneath the biological mechanisms of addictions are psychological undercurrents such as loneliness, perfectionism and a thirst for healthy relationships.

Therefore, a robust inner life of feelings and thoughts is there to enrich your life and guide you. But in order for this to work you have to pursue awareness of it and embrace it.

There is another supremely important value in accepting our feelings beyond the hidden wisdom that can be valuable if only we would learn to listen to our feelings. The feelings we have occur to us so naturally and spontaneously because they are expressions of who we are. When you neglect your feelings, you neglect yourself. When you recognize and honor your feelings, you feel your authentic self.

So much childhood pain that remains into adulthood can be traced back to times when a person's natural feelings were not being attended to or were downright devalued. It has been noted by many that in fact the impact of emotional neglect is far more insidious than physical abuse. The reason for this is because when a person's feelings are neglected their very sense existence is not validated. Many people seem perfect on the outside, but on the inside they wonder if they matter, they doubt their existence to be like "everyone else," and really don't believe they are inherently worthy. All this because others neglected their feelings when they were young.

Childhood emotional neglect leaves a tell-tale finger print. In fact, many times when a person is dealing with anxiety, or depression or low self-esteem, when we begin to explore the psychological roots of what is going on for them, we discover that they are really dealing with the aftermath of emotional neglect from childhood.

Signs that someone is being held back in life because of childhood emotional neglect include:

- A feeling of not mattering
- Not being able to remember any obvious abuse
- Thoughts like: Feelings don't matter, I just need to get over it.
- Believing that there is "something" inherently wrong or different about you that makes you inferior.
- Feeling empty or hollow inside
- Feeling emotional, but not being able to identify what you are feeling in the moment

The overall sense an adult has when he was emotionally neglected as a child is that he does not have a strong sense of self. He doesn't notice his own feelings, he fails to act in his own interest, he neglects to give compassion and attention to what he sense intuitively.

So as not to perpetuate this dynamic, it is important to personally acknowledge and accept your feelings. As you learn to do this in therapy, you get more in touch with your authentic self and learn how to relate to others with self-respect. Often times, anxiety and depression and other issues that bring us to therapy are symptoms that arise because we are suppressing our feelings which actually threatens our sense of having a self. For this reason, when you learn to open up to your feelings, you will most naturally experience a reduction of anxiety and depression.

Feelings can alert you to important messages in your life and they also represent your authentic self. For these two reasons, feelings tend to be at the center stage of therapy. So, now that you know how important feelings are in therapy and life, how does that make you feel?

CHAPTER 5

MAKING THERAPY WORK OUTSIDE OF THE SESSION

Start With the End In Mind

One of the most important steps in self-improvement and change is to start with the end in mind. It's good to think about how things can be and hope you would like them to be. Sometimes, we get so used to our suffering that we give up hope and lose sight of ever making things better. When this happens, instead of trying to improve things, we end up just complaining about how bad they are.

None of this is conscious, and no one purposely gives up and surrenders to a life of misery. However, when you come to a point in life when you've had enough and you really want to get better, the first step is to re-engage your imagination. Imagine what your best possible outcome would be! For now, you don't have to set any goals, you don't even have to believe that you're going to achieve it. But you have to be able to imagine it just to get your mind out of the complacent complaining state and prepare yourself to succeed.

You can think about it now, even as you are reading this, what would your ideal life and recovery look like?

Therapy is not the goal, it is merely something helpful to you to have a better life. The goal will include something like to have a better sense of self, a better relationship with your spouse, family and friends. Maybe you want to do something meaningful for both yourself and others. Keeping these goals in mind orient your therapy and motivate you.

Being Active Outside of Therapy

Therapy is not the goal, and so it's not enough to just be active in therapy during the session. Part of making therapy work means being active outside of the sessions as well. For each individual, this means something else personal to them. Below I list some popular options that have been helpful to many people so that you can explore if it speaks to you:

Meditation- There are many different forms of meditation, but the number one growing in popularity is Mindfulness meditation. Mindfulness is a form of meditation that has been shown to dramatically help people who are suffering with chronic pain, anxiety, depression and addictions. Honestly, in the opinion of this writer, it's one of the best ways to learn how to deal with the stress of daily living. And what's great about it is that training in this form of meditation is easily accessible to almost anyone. You can search for local trainers, or download any number of free apps that teach it to you. I often recommend Headspace app. This is a real easy way to get started and the benefits are immense!

Yoga- Research keeps coming in consistently that talk therapy is not enough. For a full recovery, a person benefits from activities that incorporate using the body. Yoga helps calm the mind and the body. Some describe it as a form or meditation while others consider it exercise. Yoga helps put you in touch with your body and stay present. This is a great way to add to your healing and personal growth.

Fitness/Exercise- A healthy body is a healthy mind! This is true at so many levels. Firstly, it's hard to feel good if your body doesn't feel good. Put yourself back in shape and increase your energy level. Secondly, when you exercise, you release a cascade of healthy endorphins and other natural chemicals which for some can be as powerful as taking antidepressants- just without any side effects.

Journaling- Journaling can be done in an unstructured way by just writing about whatever is on your mind or what happened that day. Alternatively, there are many different exercises you can do that guide you in exploring yourself and life in helpful ways. I often recommend to my clients that they buy a diary dedicated for reflecting on their sessions throughout the week. Resources for journaling can be found in the library, online, or by asking your therapist. One outstanding resource is a journaling book by Lisa Ferentz called "Finding Your Ruby Slippers." What I love about this particular book is that in addition to journaling prompts, each chapter has a nugget of wisdom. Books like this are strong sources of psychospiritual nourishment and worth keeping on your night table.

Reading/Bibliotherapy- is anything included in your own research about your betterment. This can include reading books from the library, googling whatever is your interest, and even seeking out any and all resources that may be helpful to you. For example, if you are struggling with parenting, there are almost endless amounts of great resources online and in person from the bookstore and library, to local trainings and support groups. Whatever you're struggling with it, you're not alone- or at least you don't have to be. You just need to reach out and find other people who may be there or have been there that you can connect with and learn from. This can be great for you and imagine how much you can be helpful to others!

Therapy Isn't 1-Hour a Week

There are two ways that the therapy session can produce positive change in your life. The first is transformational change which refers to any process that in the immediate moment of therapy activates an emotional healing. The other type of change is one that offers you direction and insight into growing into better health. These two actions of Healing and Growing are the major goals of almost all therapies.

When healing occurs through transformational change, it occurs in the hour of the therapy session. However, the majority of the time, change only occurs through a growing process that happens both in the session and out. How you integrate your therapy session into the rest of your life will be a big deciding factor in how effective your therapy will be.

Sometimes, especially after what feels like a good therapy session, you may find yourself asking, "Ok, so now what?" There's a certain part of us that almost expects change to happen by itself. Remember what we said above that the major goal of therapy is to help shift to a sense of empowerment. That means that even after participating actively and with motivation in therapy, you have to keep that activity up outside of the session as well. Change will not happen just from talking about it in session with your therapist. You will have to make the change. You will have to choose to make that change.

If you are at a point in your therapy when you are thinking about asking, "When will therapy work already?" I offer you the answer: "Never." Therapy never works, you have to follow through in some way or another to carry out the changes that you are seeking.

For example, let's say you are working on an internalized belief that you will never be appreciated for your hard work. In therapy, you may have done some exploration work to discover this limiting belief. You may have even discovered that you especially feel this in the context of making money. For a small group of people, just having this insight is enough to produce spontaneous changes that they will no longer be expecting others to not appreciate them. However, many times this change doesn't emerge on its own. When this happens, you need to hold on to this new knowledge and then find a time in the week to apply it. This requires three steps:

1. Slowing down

2. Awareness

3. Choice

Slowing down refers to being more attuned to your moment-to-moment experience and checking in with yourself to understand what you're feeling. At any point in the day or week that you are feeling anything at all, it's good to just check in with yourself curiously to understand what you are feeling and why.

Awareness means that at some time in the week you apply the self-knowledge that you developed in session to something occurring in your life. Usually, you apply it to something that enters your awareness after you slowed down. Using the example above, perhaps you find yourself not applying for a promotion because you don't believe that your boss will consider you a hard worker and a decent candidate. In the moment that you catch yourself avoiding the opportunity, you then recognize it as another matter being motivated by your limiting belief that you won't be appreciated. When you bring your self-knowledge to a place of present awareness, you shift from knowing to experiencing. That shift creates an opportunity to change the course of events by making a choice.

Choosing means that you intentionally take action based on your values in the direction of the change you want to make. So long as your limiting belief operates below the level of consciousness, you are not in the position to choose, but instead are on somewhat of an auto-drive. However, once you are in a state of awareness, although you will still be facing a drive compelling you to avoid the pain of being rejected and feeling unappreciated, you will be in a position to actually choose to go against that reflex. Of course this choice can be difficult and uncomfortable, but in the long run, it will be well worth the willingness to try.

It would be incomplete to omit the timeless words of wisdom of Viktor Frankl who wrote in Man's Search For Meaning, [6] "Between stimulus and response there is a space. In

---

[6] Viktor Frankl was a Jewish psychiatrist who developed a psychological theory called Logotherapy. His theory on the role of Man's pursuit of purpose was influenced by his own experiences surviving the Holocaust.

that space is our power to choose our response. In our response lies our growth and our freedom."

In this way, you will be extending the work you do in therapy into the rest of your week and integrating it into your developing self. This certainly requires motivation, but contributes to successfully healing and growing in therapy. Clients who garner their own proactive self-efficacy to make intentional choices outside of therapy are doing their part to make therapy work.

Michael Elliot

CHAPTER 6

HOW THE THERAPEUTIC RELATIONSHIP
MAKES THERAPY WORK

I'm not sure if there is any other topic in the field of therapy that draws more interest and conversation (er, intrigue and controversy) than that of the therapeutic relationship.

In their book, The Heart and Soul of Change, Psychotherapy researchers Hubble and Miller, reported from the research that one of the biggest factors in the success of therapy is not the particular technique or theory, but rather the actual therapeutic relationship. This is something that should seem intuitively obvious because if there is no safe and positive relationship between therapist and client, how can the client be expected to find healing from past wounds- many of which have been inflicted in the context of a relationship?

However, what is of particular interest in their research is that it wasn't sufficient for the therapist to provide the conditions of a good relationship such as positive regard, empathy, and good listening. What mattered most was whether the client perceived the relationship in a good way.

There is no one-size-fits-all description of the perfect therapeutic relationship. For some, it requires only that they have a good collaborative working relationship focused on the therapeutic task in the context of empathy and confidentiality. For others, it requires a deeper sense of being cared for and attachment. The rule of thumb to keep in mind is to allow yourself to have an authentic relationship with the therapist and allow that relationship to develop on its own. If you are naturally finding yourself attaching to your therapist, then notice it, and let it in.

Clients sometimes have a hard time looking at the relationship with the therapist as a positive one. Below I talk about some myths and common questions that clients ask (or want to ask) that can hold them back from connecting with the therapist and viewing the relationship as positive. I have organized these points in Q&A format because this is how they usually come up.

The Therapist Doesn't Really Care About Me, It's Just Their Job.

Nope! The therapist actually chose this job because he cares. All the therapists that I personally know are caring and compassionate people and that's exactly what drew them into the helping profession. This is really no different than a teacher that cares about her students.

Furthermore, caring is a human emotion, it just shows up when it does. When it doesn't, there's not much to do about it except maybe look at some reasons why it's not there.

When a person is sitting across from their therapist who actually cares about her, she doesn't have to think about it, but can authentically feel it. But what happens is we deny that feeling that we sense because there's something blocking us from feeling comfortable with it. If you are struggling to acknowledge your therapist's genuine care for you, perhaps you can look at what factors might be contributing to making it difficult to acknowledge. For example, consider what would it mean to you if you did believe that your therapist genuinely cared for you? Would it be uncomfortable for you? Would it be disappointing that it's not enough? Or perhaps you would lose a sense of pride for being a loner? What do you think?

I Don't Want To Connect To the Therapist, I Want a Real Relationship.

You are correct to want that!

The point of therapy is to help you develop in a way that you can do well outside of therapy sessions and the therapy relationship. Opening up to the therapist and connecting to her won't cause you to stop pursuing a satisfying relationship in your life. For most people, it helps them.

The truth is, the therapeutic relationship is a relationship to help you grow and develop in your own way. However, it isn't a model relationship for marriage or friendship. In marriage, friendships and other relationships, a healthy dynamic would be one in which both parties show mutual attention to the other with reciprocity. The therapeutic relationship is the only relationship that is all about you. The reason for this is that the therapeutic relationship is there for you to grow and be a healthy individual. In contrast, in your other relationships such as friendships and marriage it's the opposite.

Your ability to be a healthy individual serves the purpose of creating a beautiful relationship.

If The Therapist Genuinely Cares and Means What She Says, Why Is She Taking Money For It?

You aren't paying for care and connection. You are paying for time, expertise, and experience. You are also paying for the therapist to be authentic, and that means she won't be pretending to care just to make you feel good.

It can sometimes be upsetting, if not downright demoralizing, when a person feels she has to pay for someone to care enough to help her develop a sense of self and validity. Many people resent that this basic human need wasn't given to them in life by their parents, friends and loved ones. Nothing can justify the fact that a person was subjected to the pain of loneliness or neglect.

On the other hand, if you are currently in therapy, you have a lot to be proud of. You are fighting for yourself and investing in your recovery, your loved ones, and your children.

Brooke was a 21 year old single woman who was self-referred to therapy to address unresolved tensions about her father who disappeared when she was 5 only to reappear when she was 19. One day, before she left the office, I asked her if she wanted to use the back door to avoid seeing anyone in the waiting room. Her response said a lot about her character. She said, "I have nothing to be embarrassed about. My father, he should be embarrassed for not being there for me. But I'm proud of myself because I'm taking care of myself!"

The Therapist Is Fake, and I Don't Want To Need Him So Much!

This is a concern I hear on such a frequent basis that I believe it represents something inherent to the actual therapy process. In order to get the most out of your therapy, it would be helpful to establish an authentic connection to your therapist to the point that their care actually means something to you. However, it's so hard to perceive the therapist as authentic when he isn't really in your life in an organic way. In order to be able to take in the therapist's authenticity despite the fact that the therapeutic relationship is not like any other relationship in life, it's important to understand why the terms of the therapeutic relationship are the way they are.

As we mentioned before, the sum total objective of all of therapy is to facilitate your growing from a place of powerlessness, inadequacy, and submissiveness, to a place of self-reliance, confidence and empowerment. One of the main reasons that individuals get stuck in negative patterns of emotion or behavior is because at some level they are still hoping that their needs will be met by someone else outside of them.

This unarticulated hope shows up in every interaction in their life. For example, if someone wasn't given enough attention growing up and as a child took in the lesson that they aren't important, they begin to crave recognition from other people outside of them to assure them that they are important.

What this person may not realize is that needing this from outside of them only serves to perpetuate their disempowerment and unhealthy reliance on others. Thus, even if they succeed in getting positive recognition and regard from someone else, they will only continue to crave more and feel unfulfilled, like a cup with a hole that never gets filled.

Instead, in order to move towards self-reliance and confidence you will need to learn to believe in your own worthiness. Of course, it can be helpful when your belief in yourself is affirmed by others; however, ultimately the confident person is one who believes in herself, not the one who seeks reassurance from others.

That being said, it's not the therapist's job to give the positive regard and confidence to the client, but instead to help the client generate it on their own. In order to do this successfully, the therapist does not even play the role of a natural "other" in the client's life. Instead, the therapist is an externalized representation of the client's own self work.

The therapist may offer caring and warmth, however, this won't be to serve as a source of caring for the client as much as a support and affirmation to the client's own self-care.

For this reason, the therapist's role is basically limited to the time in session. Understanding this crucial point allows you to fully take in that the therapist is not fake, but in fact very real as well as their caring and authentic fondness of you. It is for this reason that most therapists discourage contact in between sessions for therapy related issues. Similarly, most therapists also discourage texting and emails. This is not just an issue of boundaries but also a matter of good principles to help you develop your own self-reliance and confidence.

Most therapists are not sadistic people and it's against their nature to hold back any act of love and kindness. What enables therapists to do a good job at what they do, despite the fact that it goes against their nature, is that ultimately facilitating the client's self-ownership is the greatest act of kindness they can do. It's also the process of developing self-ownership that makes therapy so rewarding for the client!

But If My Problems Started Because I Wasn't Loved Enough, Don't I Need Someone Else To Love Me In Order To Heal?

Love is an important and healthy thing and it would probably suit you well to seek it. Most people don't feel fulfilled without it.

However, in terms of making your recovery, it might not be as necessary as you think. Instead of trying to seek the love you were never given, try grieving that loss and how it impacted you. Then, through that grief and acceptance, you will be in a better position to take in empathy and care from others.

Empathy and caring is not as intense as unconditional love. However, it seems that seeking the love only perpetuates the suffering of powerlessness and inadequacy, as opposed to seeking empathy and care from another person which helps you embrace self-reliance and empowerment.

Making this shift in focus from getting your needs met by others to growing to be a healthy individual with self-ownership will change the whole experience of therapy as well as help you make the change you seek in your life.

Frequently, people will imagine that getting married would solve their problems. However, keep in mind that a good marriage usually requires two healthy and stable individuals. The only problem that marriage solves is being single.

So, Basically I Should Give Up On Ever Being Important To Others, and Just Soldier It Myself? So Why Bother With Therapy?

No man is an island. It is still healthy and worthwhile to seek empathy and care. After that, when you develop a better sense of self and confidence through therapy, you will be better poised to connect to another person and find true love and healthy connection. Self-reliance is not a contradiction to being connected in a healthy way to another person. In fact, research shows that only people who develop healthy attachments to others are able to develop a healthy sense of self-reliance and individuation.

It's Not Me, It's You

Since Freud, the bedrock of therapy is a concept called transference. In short, transference refers to the fact that unresolved conflicts from childhood get stuck in the unconscious and play out in a person's life without her even knowing about it. The person experiences relationships in her present life through the distorted perception of her unresolved past. Essentially, she is transferring her past experiencing into her present perception. In therapy this will inevitably show up in the therapeutic relationship and creates an opportunity to heal it.

For this reason, even though the therapist is not the most important person in your life, your relationship with your therapist parallels your most important relationships in life. By working with your therapist and how you relate to him, you begin to understand your other relationships and heal them too.

Consider for example Mike, a 36 year old business owner. Mike heard that I specialize in helping individuals who struggle establishing or maintaining relationships and so he made an appointment to consult with me at my office. Mike described himself as never having had a long term relationship with anybody, and he really wanted to find someone with whom he connected deeply and could marry. More recently, Mike has been having angry outbursts with the women he was dating which has led him to be rude to them in ways he was ashamed about. Originally, Mike just wanted to come in for a "consultation" which he described as receiving feedback on his situation, but without his commitment to doing therapy.

I pointed out to Mike that he is trying to engage me without commitment, without investment, and without the necessary time I would need to get to know him. I explained to him that without his opening up over a period of time and getting more comfortable with me, I wouldn't be able to see the real him which means that he is asking me to relate to him at the surface-level and not at a level of depth to know the real him. I noted to myself that it is no wonder that Mike is having difficulty establishing long-term relationships since he wants to be related to as if he has no depth.

I told him that I would not be able to connect to him this way and therefore would not be able to help. Mike pushed further and insisted that I help him anyway and accused me of just sticking to policy. Again, I explained that this wasn't an issue of policy but rather a matter of fact that I couldn't change even if I wanted. How could I possibly help and relate to a person without his willingness to be known?

Mike grew increasingly more frustrated and as the session progressed, when he realized he wouldn't get his way, Mike snarled at me and said, "You therapists are all fakers, you just want me to keep coming in here forever so you can make a mint off me." At this point, it became clear to me that Mike was perceiving me through transference. It was also clear to me that Mike himself did not know that he was mis-perceiving me because of his own projections, and so I wanted to help him bring awareness to this.

I said, "Mike, notice how you get angry at me and call me a faker and try to shame me when I tell you that I can only help you if you allow me to get to know you and connect to you. What is it about me wanting to connect authentically to you that makes you feel threatened?"

Mike looked embarrassed about his angry outburst and sat back in his seat. He could hear the genuine tone in my voice. He reflected on the question and said, "I guess, I don't feel so comfortable with you getting to know me any deeper than this. I think if you got to know me better, you would think there's something wrong with me and wouldn't give me advice on how to improve my relationships because you'd think I am not worthy to be in a relationship. You'd realize there was something really wrong with me."

I could see that Mike was really receptive at this point because he took a risk by letting down his defenses and opened up to me about something going on inside of him. I inquired, "When I made myself available to connect with you, you protected yourself from me by getting angry with me and accusing me of being a faker as if I don't genuinely want to know you. You projected your fear of being rejected by me onto me and perceived me as not truly being interested in you. Is it possible that this is connected to your current dating life and how you try to establish yourself in a long-term relationship and yet have been getting angry and actually pushing away women who are interested in you?"

He said, "How could they really ever love me? If only they got to know me better, no woman could really love me."

I responded, "There is some truth to what you say. No woman could ever love you unless of course you let her try by allowing her to get to know you. Of course, you don't sound like you have been letting anyone get to know you, because you don't yet love yourself." Mike began to cry.

Mike was honestly looking to get into a long-term relationship. What he didn't realize is that he himself was making a subconscious contribution that prevented him from achieving this goal. In the context of the therapy relationship, he discovered that his own belief of not being good enough was showing up and affecting his style of relating to others. In therapy he was able to recognize how he did this automatically and this allowed him to see it as a pattern in his dating life.

Don't Disappear From Your Therapist

If you don't like your therapist, tell her. If you feel like you aren't getting anything out it, tell her. If you just think you're done with therapy, tell her.

The truth is, endings are hard for most people no matter what the relationship is. Take advantage of the fact that therapy is the only relationship that is all about you. This is an opportunity for you to have the experience of saying goodbye in a healthy way. No texting it- nice try.

The only thing harder than facing hard issues in therapy, is facing the issue of leaving therapy. Think about what you're avoiding, and try to turn it into a healthy experience. No matter what the reason, when you bring up the issue with your therapist, you end up walking away with more dignity.

To be sure, sometimes it's just time to leave your therapist. That could be for any number of reasons including, having other things going on in your life, feeling you have finished, and lastly, not clicking with your therapist. All of these are legitimate reasons to consider leaving therapy. However, it's too easy to just quit prematurely using some external excuse to cover up the fact that it's just too hard. Moreover, sometimes clients are not aware of the fact that the factors that are stalling therapy are things that can be addressed and need to be addressed. Therefore, it's always a good idea to talk about this with your therapist. Don't be afraid that your therapist will be defensive. Helping you work through your thoughts about therapy is part of the therapy itself and she is expecting you to talk about it with her. On the other hand, if she does get defensive and can't handle the threat of you leaving therapy, then at least you brought it up with her and learned that she is definitely not a good fit for you.

FINAL THOUGHTS

THERAPY IS HARD WORK, BUT REWARDING

Being in therapy is anything but easy. In fact, much of the time, provoking anxiety is actually characteristic of good therapy.

Still, therapy shouldn't feel like pure torture. If it does, it doesn't mean you should run away from it. Bring it up with your therapist and talk about it openly. The very talking about it is usually helpful and also contributes to building the therapeutic relationship which is so important to the healing.

It's also a great learning opportunity for life. Meaningful relationships require good communication and working things out collaboratively. Therapists are trained to be open and comfortable with working collaboratively. This presents you with the opportunity to learn these skills which many people didn't get from their parents growing up.

If your therapist isn't open to working collaboratively, or doesn't seem comfortable with himself, this may be a sign that he can't help you.

How Long Does Therapy Take?

The biggest question that everybody wants an answer to is how long will therapy take. To be honest, there is no one-size-fits-all response to this. The reality is that most of the symptoms that bring someone into therapy to begin with are nested in the context of their personality structure and psychological constitution. Often people will say that they prefer quick results. Usually this is a statement that is coming out of fear of the therapeutic process. However, in truth, the change you are seeking is most likely deeper than just the surface and like most people, you won't be satisfied with superficial change. That being said, it usually is not a sufficient course of treatment to just learn "life skills" to help "regulate your emotions." In my experience, the deep rewarding change that people truly seek only can happen in the unhurried environment of long term therapy.

Usually, I explain to people with whom I work that an average course of therapy is about two years. This is only an average and may give you an idea of what to expect, but should not be used as a way of determining your own length of time in therapy. Many others stay for five years and longer. Knowing this at the beginning is hard to hear, but takes a lot of pressure off both the client and therapist as therapy progresses and this truth becomes self-evident.

Do some people require only 6 months to a year? Yes, certainly. In fact, some come for much less and still reap the benefits of working at depth. It depends on what the actual goals of therapy are, and what resources like time and money are available. However, it's impossible to know ahead of time how much time therapy will take for each person. The good news is that the benefits of therapy begin to pay off in a gradual way so that you don't have to wait a full two years just to reap benefits.

The real answer is that therapy takes as long as it takes and it ends when you end it. The biggest consideration you will probably want to keep in mind is what your goals are for therapy and if you are progressing towards your goals. To consider this, you may want to view all therapy goals as fitting in one of two categories: outcome goals and process goals. Outcome goals refer to goals you have of actual changes you want to make in your life. Process goals are the objectives that you want to gain from participating in the therapy process and changing the way you relate to yourself and emotional world. These are the new ways you learn to be in the therapy process that will benefit you as they carry over to other areas in your life.

Common examples of outcome goals may include:

- Reducing anxiety and worry

- Decreasing symptoms of depression

- Gain better control of impulses like anger, and sexual behavior

- Increase positive social behavior

- Participate in more meaningful activities

- Gaining an overall sense of mastery and healthy control of your life environment

- Improve self-esteem and self-image

- Self-acceptance

Common examples of process goals include:

- Develop a greater capacity to tolerate discomfort and face difficulties

- Increase ability to self-reflect on emotions, feelings, drives and thoughts

- Learn positive attitudes towards yourself and others such as compassion

- Take ownership of your life in proactive ways by

asserting yourself, your opinions, and making better decisions

- Acceptance of reality as it is

When you achieve your goals or it becomes obvious that are not making progress in that direction, then it is time to consider leaving therapy. If you are still gaining from the therapy process, either because you are getting closer to achieving the outcomes you wanted or because you benefit from the process of therapy, then you will probably choose to continue.

Good therapy should feel positive, not because it's pleasurable, but because it's rewarding. In general, therapy is rewarding when you and your therapist are focused on challenging issues and topics and facing those topics with bravery and the intention to grow.

APPENDIX

SIMPLIFYING SELF CONFIDENCE

Self-confidence is actually pretty simple and natural; however, most people misunderstand what self-confidence is, and in doing so, true self confidence evades them. When you are not feeling confident, you may be plagued by doubts that you will ever be loved and appreciated or that you can make good decisions in governing your life. These self-doubts can cause a lot distress and pain and so naturally you begin to want to rid yourself of these doubts and want the opposite of self-doubt. The problem begins when you mistakenly think that the opposite of self-doubt is having certainty in your self. Unfortunately, Confidence based on certainty is hardly achievable. Few things in life are truly certain and so when you set Certainty as your standard for having confidence, you are setting yourself up for failure. This, then contributes to your feeling that you are somehow inadequate which reinforces your self-doubt and then perpetuates the cycle of disempowerment.

Trying to achieve Self-confidence based on certainty is a recipe for psychological disaster. Instead, consider an alternative model of self-confidence that is built on self-ownership. We often feel paralyzed from making decisions or asserting ourselves because we don't have a feeling of certainty. It is not the uncertainty in itself that paralyzes you, but the idea that you need it and that without you *can't* or *shouldn't* be confident. Ultimately, you must come to terms with the fact that engaging in a meaningful life requires you to make decisions without actually knowing if they are right. Therefore, it's really important to *let go* of your unrelenting standard requiring certainty. When you let go of that need for certainty and come to terms with the fact that it is truly unachievable, you allow yourself to make decisions based on the fact that your life is yours and you have to make decisions with or without certainty. That is what it means to have a healthy self-confidence based on owning your life and living it!

You develop more confidence not because you know you are right, but because you value living your life as your own. One of the greatest insights people get in the work of therapy is learning that their life is theirs and only they can live it. So, at one level, the overall objective of therapy is to move in the direction of self-ownership or self-sovereignty.

As one particularly insightful client put it, "I still don't have a great deal of confidence that I know for sure what I'm doing in life; but, now I see that no one else necessarily knows any better."

WHEN YOU STILL AREN'T SURE IF THERAPY IS WORKING FOR YOU

Therapy is complicated and the journey can require the tolerating of a lot of ambiguity. It's an expected part of therapy that there are plenty of sessions and even stretches of time that it's not clear if things are going as they should. This isn't always an indication that you are off track at all. The first course of action should always be to discuss this openly with your therapist.

Over the years, I have found that it can sometimes be helpful to bring in a third party consultant who isn't part of the therapeutic dyad. This is helpful to both the client and the therapist. The consultant should be a professional clinician who is experienced in both providing treatment and supervision. This consultation can help to assess the client's needs, and whether the therapy is working or not and can also provide direction to both the client and therapist to understand what needs to be done to **make therapy work.**

If you are interested in finding a Professional Consultant that can help you make the most of your therapy or give you the direction you need in deciding whether therapy is working or not, visit us today at www.howtomaketherapywork.com or email me directly at MakingTherapyWork@Gmail.com.

ABOUT THE AUTHOR

Michael Schlein, LCPC is an author and Therapist specializing in the treatment of anxiety and depression. He has worked with patients suffering from issues ranging from low self-esteem to addictions and complex trauma. In addition to his writing and private psychotherapy practice in Baltimore, MD, he offers consultations on a broad range of therapy related topics to therapists and clients around the world. He can be reached at MakingTherapyWork@gmail.com.